THE COMPLETE GUIDE TO BECOMING A MERCHANT SEAMAN

HOW TO MAKE $5,000 TO $10,000 A MONTH WITHOUT A GED OR HIGH SCHOOL DIPLOMA

1ST EDITION
TERRANCE OMEGA JACKSON

MSC PRESS

Published in the United States by MSC Press in Charleston, SC

Library of Congress Control Number:

2021907735

ISBN 978-0-578-89618-2

First Paperback Edition

Links: We are not responsible for the availability of any other site to which this site links. We do not endorse or take responsibility for the contents, advertising, products, or other materials made available through any other site. Under no circumstances will we be held responsible or liable, directly or indirectly, for any loss or damage caused or alleged to have been caused to you in connection with your use of, or reliance on, any content, goods, or services available on any other site. You should direct any concerns to that site administrator or webmaster. We do not endorse, warrant, or guarantee any products or services offered on any third-party site. We are not a party to, and do not monitor, any transaction between users and third-party providers of products or services.

TABLE OF CONTENTS

THERE ARE MANY HELPFUL LINKS IN THIS MANUAL. YOU SHOULD READ IT ON YOUR COMPUTER OR INTERNET-CONNECTED READER SO YOU CAN REFER TO THE HELPFUL LINKS WHILE READING. SOME OF THE WEBSITE LINKS YOU WILL HAVE TO COPY THE URL AND PASTE IT IN THE WEB BROWSER TO GET THEM TO WORK.

DISCLAIMER

None of this book should be considered advice. It is purely for educational purposes.

The list below is general in detail and is an overview to what is required to become a merchant seaman.

Because the details of the rules and laws regarding how to become a merchant seaman may change at any time, it would be impossible to keep an updated list of the rules/regulations every day.

So you must review and understand the requirements that you will need in this reading as a potential merchant seaman, and you must become familiar with the details of the rules and laws of the Coastguard's NMC (National Maritime Center).

THE COMPLETE GUIDE TO BECOMING A MERCHANT SEAMAN

How to Make $5,000 to $10,000 a Month without a GED or High School Diploma

First, I want to thank you for ordering this book. You will find it a helpful introduction to becoming a merchant seaman. It's a lot of information, but don't get overwhelmed. You'll have a good understanding when finished.

Becoming a merchant seaman is a process that will take some time, money, and patience, but it is worth it when you can make $5,000 to $10,000 a month. If you are looking for a get-rich-quick approach, this isn't the book for you. However, if you are willing to put in the work and follow the simple instructions in this book, you will be well on your way to making $5,000 to $10,000 a month.

So let's get started!

WHO CAN BE A MERCHANT SEAMAN?

To become a merchant seaman, you must meet the following requirements:

- Be a US citizen or permanent resident

- Meet the United States Coast Guard's standards for medical fitness

- Be able to read, understand, and speak the English language

- Be eighteen years of age or older, of either gender. If younger than eighteen, you must have a parent or guardian's consent. However, most programs or jobs will only accept someone who is eighteen years of age or older. Even senior citizens can apply. I've worked with people that were in their sixties and seventies.

If you have been convicted of a crime, you may still be considered eligible, no matter what you've done. I've worked with people that went to jail but were still able to come out and start a career as a merchant seaman. To find out if you are eligible, call (888) 427-5662, and when prompted, press 4. Tell them, "I'm interested in becoming a merchant seaman, but I've been convicted of something. Can I still apply?" You can also go to www.ecfr.gov and scroll down to section 10.211, Criminal Record Review for more information.

WHAT IS A MERCHANT SEAMAN?

Throughout this book, you will hear the term *merchant seaman* or *merchant mariner*. They mean the same thing. But let's be clear, a merchant seaman or merchant mariner is not in any way a part of the military. Merchant seamen work on ships that provide a service or transport people or products from one place to another over a body of water. That body of water could be the Indian Ocean, the Mississippi River, canals, the Great Lakes, the Atlantic Ocean, or the Pacific Ocean. Merchant seamen service various industries and work on different sizes of vessels. Merchant mariners work on excursion vessels, charter boats, oil tankers, tugboats, container ships, ferries, towboats, dredges, and other waterborne crafts. Some ships just travel from port to port in and around the United States, and other ships travel outside the United States to other countries. The United States could not operate without merchant seamen. Merchant seamen move 75% of the United States' raw materials and goods around the world every year. Here are a couple of examples of how ships provide services:

- A cable ship lays internet cable underneath the ocean floor.
- A hospital ship provides medical care.
- A research ship does oceanic research.
- A transport ship, such as a cruise ship or ferry, transports people.
- A bulk carrier transports goods such as cement, coal, ore, and grains.

Just look around your house and pick out any item. Chances are you will find that it was not made in the United States. Take a minute and look at your car, TV, washing machine, shoes, clothes, cell phone, food, or kid's toys. Somewhere on the item, it will say where the item was made, like Japan, China, or Germany. If your car was made in Japan, a car carrier ship left the United States, went to Japan, and picked up your car to bring it back to the United States to be sold at your local dealership. If your TV was made in China, a container ship left the United States, went to China to pick up your TV, and brought it back to be sold in your local Walmart. Even the gas you use in your car was transported by ship. That means an oil tanker ship went to, let's say, Houston, Texas, picked up crude oil from one port, and then delivered that crude oil to a refinery in Jacksonville, Florida. The refinery then, through a refining process, turned that crude oil into gasoline, jet fuel, kerosene, diesel, and many other byproducts.

THE DIFFERENCE BETWEEN A LICENSED AND UNLICENSED MERCHANT SEAMAN

If you are prior military and have qualifying sea time, pay close attention to this section because you may be able to use your sea time to become an officer or one of the higher ratings above entry level. Inside your merchant seaman application packet, there is a form for you to fill out, and the Coast Guard will determine whether your sea time will be accepted or not. If you decide to go to one of the maritime colleges, you will need a high school diploma.

What's a licensed merchant seaman? A licensed merchant seaman is someone who has attended and graduated from one of the maritime colleges or apprenticeship programs for officers or has 1,080 days of approved sea time. If either of these is applicable, you can take the Coast Guard-approved tests/requirements to become a licensed merchant seaman. A licensed merchant seaman works on a ship as an officer.

If you have not attended and graduated from one of the maritime colleges or apprenticeship programs for officers or if you do not have 1,080 days of approved sea time, you are not eligible to take the Coast Guard-approved tests or fulfill the requirements to obtain a license and cannot work on ships as an officer. An unlicensed merchant seaman can work on ships under one of the unlicensed positions but not in a licensed officer position.

SOME OF THE DEPARTMENTS LICENSED AND UNLICENSED MERCHANT SEAMAN WORK IN

Unlicensed merchant seaman can work in all three departments (engine, deck, or steward), but licensed merchant seamen only work in two departments, engine or deck, as they are the only departments that have officers. Here is a brief description of each department:

- Engine Department: Members of the engine department make rounds and do preventative maintenance on the ship's engine and other machinery to ensure they work properly.

- Deck Department: Members of the deck department make sure the ship is tied and untied safely during docking and undocking. They also do preventative maintenance on the outside of the ship and are responsible for the ship's navigation, cargo, and safety.

- Steward Department: Members of the steward department work in the kitchen. They prepare and cook all the ship's meals and make sure that new merchant seamen joining the ship have clean linens, soap, and towels.

Licensed Positions

Deck Department	Engine Department
Captain	Chief Engineer
Chief Mate	First Assistant Engineer
Second Mate	Second Assistant Engineer
Third Mate	Third Assistant Engineer

Unlicensed Positions

Deck Department	Engine Department	Steward Department
Bosun	Pump Man	Steward
Able Seaman	Electrician	Chief Cook
Ordinary Seaman	QMED	Steward Assistant
	Oiler	
	Wiper	

YOUR DECISION TO GO LICENSED OR UNLICENSED

Your decision of whether or not to get a merchant seaman license really depends on your future goals. If you've done your due diligence and you think you may only want to sail four to five years and that being a merchant seaman is just an opportunity to save money to start a business, put kids through college, invest in real estate, or build your dream home, in my opinion, you should go the unlicensed route. My estimate is that starting out at entry level, you can make anywhere from $3,500 to $5,000 a month, depending on what type of ship you're on and whether you're working for a private company or union. You only have to sail deck or engine at entry level for four months, and six months for the steward department. Then you're eligible to take a Coast Guard test and fulfill the requirements to move up to a higher position. If you move out of the entry level within your first year, then within five years, you could have $100,000 in your savings account if married, $150,000–$200,000 if single. This is not a guarantee. How much you can make depends on how hard you work, the type of lifestyle you live, and the type of ships you sail. Some ships pay more than others. I can say from my experience and those of many merchant seamen I know, this is a very realistic goal.

If you've done your due diligence and you can see yourself doing this as a career, then I recommend going the licensed route. I estimate fresh out of a maritime college or an apprenticeship program for officers, a licensed merchant seaman can expect to make anywhere from $8,000 to $13,000 a month. A maritime degree will cost you anywhere from $100,000 to $150,000.

Side note: If you get student loans, I recommend paying off all student loans before you make any big purchases like a brand-new car or a house and before you invest in a 401(k). The sooner you pay off your loans, the less you will end up paying in interest. I've seen a lot of licensed merchant seaman graduate with $100,000 in student loan debt and then go out and buy a brand-new truck for $60,000, then a $250,000 house. Before you know it, here come the wife and kids. At that point you will be drowning in debt and working the rest of your life trying to pay it off. Without student loans and making $8,000 to $13,000 a month starting out, I estimate in five years you could have $200,000 in your savings if married, $250,000 if single. This is not a guarantee. Of course it depends on how hard you work, the type of lifestyle you live, and the ships you sail. Some ships pay more than others. It also depends on whether you work for a private company or a union. As a licensed merchant seaman, you only have to sail 365 days in a position before you can take a test and fulfill the requirements to move up to the next licensed position. These estimates are based off of you saving $20,000-$50,000 each year for 5 years.

Note: I'm not an accountant and I'm not giving financial advice. You need to talk to a licensed professional regarding your finances.

STARTING YOUR CAREER AS A LICENSED OR UNLICENSED MERCHANT SEAMAN

If you are starting your unlicensed career at entry level with limited to no maritime experience. Here is where you can start:

- **MSC (Military Sealift Command)**

  For more details call toll free: 877-JOBS-MSC (562-7672), email: civmar@sealiftcommand.com, or go to the website at https://sealiftcommand.com and click on the Entry Level icon.

- **Tankerman Career Academy:** For more details, go to the website: www.tcainfo.com.

- **SIU (Seafarers International Union):** They have a free apprenticeship program. For details call (301) 994-0010 or go to the website: www.seafarers.org. If you choose not to go through the apprenticeship program, you can still join SIU but only as a C card. The union members have a seniority structure, A, B, C. This route is harder, but it is possible. Go to the seafarers' link above and click on the heading labeled SIU Union Halls and call or stop by any one of the SIU hiring halls and say, "Hello, ma'am or sir, I would like information about joining the union as a C card."

- **SUP (Sailors' Union of the Pacific):** For more details call (415) 777-3400 or go to www.sailors.org.

- **JOBCORP:** For more details call <u>800-733-5627</u> or <u>877-889-5627</u> TTY or go to <u>https://jobcorps.gov/train/392/transportation/209/seamanship</u>.

- **MFOW (Marine Firemen's Union):** For more details call (415) 362-4592, (415) 362-4593, or (415) 362-4594 or go to <u>https://mfoww.org/</u>

- **Military To Mariner Program:** For more details call (202) 366-4000) ask to be connected to the office of public affairs. Or go to <u>https://www.maritime.dot.gov/outreach/military-mariner</u>

- **IBU (Inland Boat Men's Union):** For more details call (206) 284-6001or go to <u>https://ibu.org/maritime-jobs</u>.

If you are starting your career as a licensed merchant seaman, here is a list of colleges and some programs where you can start:

- **US Merchant Marine Academy:** For more details call (516) 726-5800 or go to the website: <u>www.usmma.edu</u>.

- **California Maritime Academy:** For more details call (707) 654-1330 or go to the website: <u>www.csum.edu</u>.

- **Massachusetts Maritime Academy:** For more details call (800) 544-3411 or go to the website: <u>www.maritime.edu</u>.

- **Texas A&M University at Galveston:** For more details call (409) 740-4706 or go to the website: <u>www.tamug.edu</u>.

- **Great Lakes Maritime Academy:** For more details call <u>(231) 995-1200</u> or go to the website: <u>www.nmc.edu</u>.

- **Maine Maritime Academy:** For more details call (207) 326-4311 or go to the website: https://mainemaritime.edu.

- **AMO Tech Program:** For more details go to the website: https://www.star-center.com/techprogram/tech.trifold.pdf or email: tech@star-center.com.

- **MITAG (Maritime Institute of Technology and Graduate Studies):** For more details call 1-888-253-8869 or go to the website: www.mitags.org. Currently this program is only for those interested in going into the deck department.

As a license merchant seaman you have the option of working for a private company, union, or you can choose to receive a commission as an ensign in the U.S. Naval Reserve, Merchant Marine Reserve, or U.S. Coast Guard Reserve.

List of License Merchant Seaman Unions

- **MM&P (Masters, Mates & Pilots):** For more details call (410) 691-8151 or go to the website: https://bridgedeck.org/. This union is only for license deck officers.

- **MEBA (Marine Engineers' Beneficial Association)** For more details call (202-638-5355) or go to the website: http://www.mebaunion.org/

- **AMO (American Maritime Officers)** For more details call (954) 921-2221/(800 362-0513 or go to the website https://www.amo-union.org/

List of Private Companies

Seabulk: www.seabulktowing.com

Superior Energy: www.superiorenergy.com

Diamond Offshore: www.diamondoffshore.com

Seadrill: www.seadrill.com

Trans Ocean : www.deepwater.com

Helix Energy Solutions: www.helixesg.com

Pacific Drilling: www.pacificdrilling.com

Maersk Drilling: www.maerskdrilling.com

Edison Chouest Offshore: www.chouest.com

Polar Tanker Inc: https://alaska.conocophillips.com/who-we-are/alaska-operations/polar-tankers-us-west-coast/

Chevron: https://www.chevron.com/operations/transportation/shipping

OSG: https://www.osg.com/corporate-profile/default.aspx

FEES

There are some fees you will have to pay in order to become a merchant seaman. Some of these fees maybe a little bit more or less depending on where you live.

- TWIC (Transportation Workers Identification Credential): $125
- MMC (Merchant Mariner Credential): $140
- Medical Certificate: $150
- Drug Test: $90
- Passport: $140

The fees below only apply to some programs. If you're not entering a program that requires them, don't worry about these fees. These figures could vary depending on what school you attend:

- STCW Basic Training endorsement: $800
- STCW Vessel Personnel with designated security duties: $230
- STCW Security Awareness with security duties: $230

DOCUMENTS & ENDORSEMENTS YOU NEED AND HOW TO OBTAIN THEM

When becoming a merchant seaman, you will possibly need the following:

- TWIC (Transportation Workers Identification Credential)
- Medical certificate
- MMC (Merchant Mariner Credential)
- Drug test
- USA passport

If you decide to take the route to become a licensed merchant seaman, your maritime college/apprenticeship program will assist you with acquiring these documents. Always check with your program before you start to find out what is needed. If after contacting your program you still need these five documents or the three additional endorsements, revert back to this section.

If you've decided to take the unlicensed merchant seaman route, continue reading, because in addition to the five documents mentioned above, some programs require you to have three additional endorsements as well. If you're not entering a program that requires the three additional endorsements, don't worry about them. Always check with your program before you start, to find out what is needed.

- STCW Basic Training endorsement
- STCW Vessel Personnel with designated security duties
- STCW Security Awareness with security duties

I will explain how to obtain each document/endorsement.

Applying for a TWIC is easy:

1. All you have to do is pick up the phone and say, "Hello, ma'am or sir, I would like to apply for a TWIC Card as part of the Merchant Mariner Credentialing process. Yes, it's just that simple: pick up the phone and call (855) 347-8371. Listen and press prompt number 2. They're open 8:00 a.m. to 10:00 p.m. Monday through Friday Eastern Standard Time. Or here is the website if you choose to fill out the application online: https://universalenroll.dhs.gov. Make sure to click on the TWIC icon with a picture of a ship in the background and answer yes when asked if you are applying for a TWIC as a part of the Merchant Mariner Credentialing.

2. Pick up the phone again and call the Coast Guard National Maritime Center at (888) 427-5662. Listen, and when prompted, press number 3.You can receive your merchant mariner application in three ways. (1) You can go online to www.uscg.mil/nmc and on the left side of the screen click on Merchant Mariner Credentialing. (2) You can have the application emailed to you. (3) You can have it physically mailed to you. If you choose to have the application emailed or mailed out to you, then you will need to leave a voice message. You will be asked to state your email address or your home mailing address, including state, city, and zip code. You will also be asked your phone number, name, social security number, or merchant mariner reference number. Your merchant mariner reference number is your social security number. If you ever call in for help, this is what they use to look up your information.

If you're taking the licensed merchant seaman route, then you have to state, "I'm applying for an original student observer, apprentice mate, or apprentice engineer position." If you've decided to start your career as an unlicensed merchant seaman, you will have to state that you're applying as an original entry-level rating. *Original* means this is the first time you're applying for a merchant mariner credential, and *entry level* means that at this time you don't have enough education, training, or sea time to work in any other positions outside of entry level. *Rating* can be described as your qualification, position, or job title. Entry level has three ratings/positions: ordinary seaman, wiper, and steward department (FH). FH stands for food handler. If you have qualifying sea time and have met all the requirements needed for that rating, you can apply for a rating higher than entry level. Once you receive the application, take your time and fill it out. If you have any, and I mean any, questions at all, dial the National Maritime Center number above. Someone will gladly answer your questions. That's their job, to help you. Once you receive your packet, fill out form CG-719B Application for Merchant Mariner Credential. Anyone that has been charged with or committed a crime, fill out form CG-719C. In order to get your medical certificate, fill out form CG-719K Application for Medical Certificate or CG-719K/E Application for Medical Certificate for Entry Level Ratings.

You will also need to fill out form CG-719P for your drug test. Last but not least, you will need a United States of America passport.

You can go online and apply at https://travel.state.gov/content/travel/en/passports/how-apply.html.

You can also go to your local post office and ask for an application for a passport.

For a list of STCW Basic Training endorsement schools, go to https://sealiftcommand.com/resources/training-school-search. Under course type, click on Firefighting and STCW Classes. Then in the next drop-down box, you will see STCW Basic Training.

For a list of STCW Vessel Personnel with Designated Security Duties and Security Awareness with Security Duties endorsement schools, go to https://sealiftcommand.com/resources/training-school-search. Under Course Type, click on Miscellaneous Courses. Then, in the next drop-down box, you will see both endorsements: Vessel Personnel with Designated Security Duties and Vessel Security Awareness with Security Duties.

TESTIMONIES

"Sailing saved my life and created stability for my family."
—Peter J., 2/AE, Jacksonville, FL

"This industry has given me the opportunity to travel to places I had never been before. Before I got into this industry, I had never even left my state."
—Terry B., Oiler, Houston, TX

"Being a merchant seaman gives me an opportunity to make a lot of money in a short amount of time and has given me the opportunity to start investing in the stock market."
—Brittany S., Chief Cook, Charleston, WV

"Through hard work and sacrifice, I was able to purchase my first rental property and at the same time provide medical benefits for me and my family."
—Eddie S., Bosun, San Juan, Puerto Rico

"I was living paycheck to paycheck, drowning in credit card and student loan debt. After becoming a merchant seaman, I have paid off all of my credit cards, and I'm slowly paying off all of my student loans."
—Nathaniel H., Wiper, Ft. Lauderdale, FL

"I was born in Zambia, Africa, and I came to the US as a student and later became a permanent resident. I became a merchant seaman, and it put me in a better position to take care of my expenses here in the US and still have enough money left over to send back to my family in Zambia."
—Rahamani B., Pumpman, Shawnee, Kansas

www.ingramcontent.com/pod-product-compliance
Lightning Source LLC
Chambersburg PA
CBHW071116090426
42737CB00013B/2600